For a better life
Faith

A Book on Self-Empowerment

Compiled by
M. M. Walia

NEW DAWN PRESS, INC.
USA • UK • INDIA

Faith is to believe
what we do not see,
and the reward of this faith is to see what
we believe.

— St Augustine

Faith is the substance of things hoped for,
the evidence of things not seen.

— Hebrews XI

Faith is an oasis in the heart
which will never be reached by the caravan
of thinking.
— Kahlil Gibran

Faith in God
and faith in ourselves
is the secret of greatness.
Losing faith in one's self
means losing faith in God.
— Swami Vivekananda

other. The faculty of pure reasoning leads us to knowledge and knowledge gives us faith.

- ❖ Perhaps we can make it clearer by relating it to our everyday experience. Sometimes we gain information through a trustworthy source and we are willing to make further inquiries about the matter. But if the same information is given to us by an untrustworthy source, we make no further inquiry.

- So, first we believe because the source is trustworthy; then we exert our reasoning faculty; we strive and inquire, and as a result of this, we gain true knowledge of the subject.
- Our devotion to higher ideals of life, or our lack of it, is related to where we place our trust. For instance, when a person is ill, he calls a physician because he has faith in the power of the physician to cure him. Whenever we are in need of human assistance, we call on those who can fulfil our

❖ Divinity is ever present in every heart, but through our critical attitude and doubting mind we often deprive ourselves of its beneficent presence. Sri Ramakrishna used to say that one finds God very directly and simply through faith; intellectual arguments only drive Him further and further away. How often had Christ said : "As ye believe, so will it be." A man of faith constructs something beautiful even in the midst of chaos, while one of doubting mind always destroys even that which has been created for his happiness.

— *Swami Paramananda*

The Basics of Faith

"Threefold is by nature the inborn faith of the embodied — the good, the passionate and the dull. The faith of each is shaped to his own nature, O Bharata, the man consists of his faith; that which his faith is, he is verily that."

— *Bhagavad Gita*

To say that the faith of each is shaped to his own nature is to indicate that the basis of faith changes according to the growth of the individual. It is faith that makes the character of a man. Man's growth is determined by the category of faith that he espouses.

The dull are those whose minds have not awakened—they suffer from mental inertia and lethargy. Their faith has a basis of fear in it. These men worship spirits and ghosts. This is indicative of fear which is born of ignorance.

The "passionate" or those moved by *rajas* are active and restless for they are moved by the intellect. The intellect is very often clever and unscrupulous. There is no wonder that the passionate worship the demons. The Faith of the passionate is faith in themselves—in the power of the intellect, in the cleverness of the mind.

The "good" worship God—they are the worshippers of the beneficent forces. They have faith. For, is not innocence the very basis of goodness? They are innocent because they are freed from the pride of mind's knowledge.

But what indeed is faith? It is a surrender to the Unknown. Faith has no relevance in terms of the known. With reference to the known one can speak of belief. If the man of faith obtains wisdom, then he is the one who has come face to face with the Unknown.

All doubts have their roots in fear. Among the many fears, there is nothing so overpowering as the fear of losing the known. But unless the known is given up, the Unknown cannot be seen, and it is the Unknown which is the begetter of faith.

Sri Krishna tells Arjuna : 'Cut asunder all doubts with the sword of wisdom', so that you may become a man inspired by faith, ready to accept the challenges of life. If we could cut asunder all doubts, then we too would become men filled with faith.

— *Shri Rohit Mehta*

Doubt – A Negative Phenomenon

Turn unto the Lord with all thy heart and ask of him without doubting, and Thou shall know the mercy of the Lord; know that He will not forsake thee, but will fulfil the request of thy soul.

– *Shepherd of Hermes*

Faith in Divine Powers

❖ In this age of materialism, it is most inspiring to see a man who is willing to face any difficulty, to lay down his life for the sake of his Ideal. The skeptical man of the world has neither the spiritual insight nor the patience to wait, and he who will not wait for the cosmic law to work out, always perishes.

❖ The man who is full of faith in the Divine, does not work for self-gratification. He has a larger point of view. He works for humanity. He has learned to offer himself in perfect faith, and no matter in what circumstances he is placed, he never forgets that his life belongs only to that One. The man who stands on this rock of truth is unshakable. He is no longer connected with the small and the personal; he has connected himself with the cosmic force; he has set his faith right and because of that he has become invincible.

❖ But placing our faith in God does not mean that we are going to eliminate all our troubles and tribulations. On the contrary, our test may be greater than that of others. We should be very glad to have hardships placed upon us so that we may prove our faith.

❖ People who lack faith are, as a rule, always faint-hearted. Whenever difficulty comes or too much is demanded of them, they give way.

❖ A man who has no faith in his own divine heritage cannot have faith in God; and a man who has no faith either in God or in himself certainly cannot have faith in humanity. Men grow suspicious of each other and this suspicion is not limited to a community or a country, it becomes a world-wide disease resulting in war, intolerance and all kinds of hideous conditions.

❖ The degradation of the individual begins when he loses faith in the power of God and no longer believes that he has any access to Divinity. As soon as man doubts himself, he lowers his standard and becomes incapable of doing anything good or noble.

Scepticism

❖ The doubt which leads us to investigate is all right; but when by the light of our soul we gain some deeper revelation, then we must throw doubt away. There are people who seem to be naturally sceptical; but their scepticism is nothing but a habit which they have cultivated and it can be replaced by another more constructive habit.

❖ Some of us take pride in our sceptical attitude. We say, we cannot accept what cannot be proved by the senses; but if we reject everything not proved by our sense-perceptions, we would reject a large part of the world.

Doubt – An Antonym of Faith

❖ Unless we have faith, we cannot work well, because doubt scatters and dissipates our energy. A little doubt enters our mind and soon a great storm is raging inside, which leaves us defected and exhausted. Doubt always tears down, it is wasteful and destructive; while faith is constructive. It is so easy to doubt; for as soon as we begin to doubt one thing, that leads to doubt of everything.

❖ When we doubt, we strike a death-blow at the very root of the tree of our life, and naturally all the leaves and flowers fade away. "The ignorant, the faithless and one of doubting mind perishes. There is neither this world, nor the next, nor any happiness for the doubting self," the *Bhagavad Gita* declares.

Utility of Doubt

❖ The enemy of faith is doubt, and yet doubt too, is a necessity and has its uses. Man in his ignorance and in his progressive labour towards knowledge needs to be visited by doubt, otherwise he would remain obstinate in limited knowledge and an ignorant belief and unable to escape from his errors.

❖ We carry with us a number of intellectual beliefs and ideas which are by no means all correct and perfect. A host of new ideas and suggestions meet us afterwards demanding our credence which would be fatal to seize upon and always cling to in the shape in which they come, without regard to their possible error, limitation or imperfection.

❖ And yet, faith is necessary throughout and at every step, because it is a needed assent of the soul, and without this assent there can be no progress.

❖ Faith is indispensable to man, for, without it he could not proceed forward in his journey through the Unknown; but it ought not to be imposed; it should come as a free perception or an imperative direction from the inner spirit. The merely sceptical mind loses itself in the void. And even a blind and ignorant faith is a better possession than sceptical doubt.

❖ It is not necessary that all doubts should disappear right in the beginning — that would make *sadhana* impossible, for doubt is the mind's persistent assailant. Do not allow the assailant to become a companion; do not give him the open door and the fireside seat.

❖ It is because our ideas and our will are in a constant state of flux or of oscillation that we do not succeed. Even with a deficient faith, a fixed mind and strong will can carry one on and bring the experiences by which an uncertain faith is changed into certitude.

❖ A doubting mind is a diseased mind. We are neither able to receive a blessing nor to retain it so long as our mind is full of doubt and despair.

— *Sri Aurobindo*

- ❖ Like a bird that pauses in his flight upon a bough too slight, feels it give way beneath him, yet he sings, knowing he hath wings.

  – Victor Hugo

- ❖ The soul of a man is forever tormented between what is legally right and morally wrong, politically shrewd and spiritually stupid – profitable for a moment but lost in eternity."

  – Dr Joseph Robert

❖ There is no such thing as partial faith. It must be total as the faith of a child in his parents.

— *Anon*

Faith and Optimism

Blind faith is the only kind to have, for faith is either blind or it is not faith but something else—reasoned inference, proved conviction or ascertained knowledge.

— *Sri Ramakrishna*

❖ One cannot have faith without optimism. Faith and hope are inseparable. Depression is a great obstacle in the spiritual life and we must strive to conquer it. People who are morose will find it very difficult to advance. Cheerfulness is one of the essential spiritual qualities. We must guard ourselves against dejection, self-denunciation, or even feeling a little down-hearted.

❖ Dejection invariably distorts our vision. It magnifies our troubles. It makes every obstacle look insurmountable. That is why in the *Bhagavad Gita*, Sri Krishna tells Arjuna that he who wishes to save himself must never allow depression to possess his mind. If he does, he becomes his own greatest enemy.

❖ Sometimes this depression is physical, sometimes it is mental, and sometimes it is spiritual. Doubt in regard to our ideals, and lack of trust in God, are forms of spiritual depression and they demoralise our life very quickly. The more active we are on the spiritual plane, the less susceptible we shall be to these dark hours of doubt.

❖ A life which is based on true faith is bound to bring great blessings and to manifest great spiritual powers. We cannot expect to gain such unbroken, unwavering faith at once; but if we seek and pray and really yearn for it from the depths of our being, the way will open by which we shall inherit this rare spiritual gift. When it comes, it will lead us to that realm of reality which never fails, which never deceives, which is more real than this world, and which is the very foundation of our being.

Blind Faith

❖ The idea of faith is often misunderstood by people, because they associate it with those who are ignorant, uneducated, and who have no power to investigate for themselves. Otherwise, if we merely believe without knowing, we are no better than the parrot who may be taught to repeat holy names, but who, as soon as it sees a cat approaching, forgets everything and only utters its natural cry.

❖ We must become more trusting in God and we must have greater faith in ourselves. We must cease to put our trust in things which are fleeting and perishable. At every step in our life let us use discrimination, let all our actions be guided not by impulse but by wisdom, and let us seek that wisdom from the Infinite Source.

Allah is the Protecting Friend of those who believe. He bringeth them out of darkness into light.

— The Quran 11.257

There is no faith without submission, and no submission without faith.

— Abu Hanifah

Faith and Self-Reliance

"Raise Yourself by Yourself, do not let Yourself down; for you are your own friend, you are your enemy."

– *The Bhagavad Gita*

❖ The *Bhagavad Gita* says that the man of unflinching faith who has mastered his senses attains wisdom, and having attained wisdom, he enjoys supreme peace; but for the one who lacks faith there is happiness neither in this world nor the next, because he destroys his own happiness by his doubting nature.

❖ True self-reliance does not mean reliance on one's physical strength; it means reliance on something mightier, something which is less perishable.

❖ The Sanskrit term *Shraddha* has a more comprehensive meaning than the English word faith; it means a sense of trust in one's higher Self, in that which is more than body and which sustains the body.

- True discrimination alone can show the way to true self-reliance, and also, it alone gives us true faith. Do not imagine that any one can have true faith in God who has no faith in himself.

- Self-reliance does not mean arrogance; on the contrary, it may mean exceeding humility. Arrogance is the result of ignorance or the identification of the self with the body and with physical conditions; whereas the truly self-reliant man is one who has faith in his divine nature only, and, therefore, he can face even death without being moved, or frightened.

❖ As we go on praying and surrendering, and learn through success and failure, happiness and misery, we realise that we cannot depend on our own strength, but that there is some-power behind us by whose will everything happens in this universe, we grow wise and decide to give up, saying, "Not my will, but Thine be done."

❖ Self-reliance is not egotism. It means trusting in the spiritual, having more faith in that which is imperishable and less in fleeting things. Such self-reliance, however, is only possible for the man who follows the path of righteousness. It is only as we awaken the latent Divinity within us and come to know our higher self that we gain true faith.

Faith

Behold, we know not anything;

I can but trust that good shall fall

At last – far off – at last, to all,

And every winter change to spring.

So runs my dreams

But what am I?
An infant crying in the night;
An infant crying for the light;
And with no language but a cry!

— *In Memoriam*
Tennyson

❖ The *Gita* tells us that this *Purusha*, this soul in man, is, as it were, made of "*shraddha*", a faith, a will to be, a belief in itself and existence, and whatever is that will, faith or constituting belief in him, he is that and that is he.

❖ Faith is the first condition of success in every great undertaking. It is no exaggeration to say that faith can move mountains. It is faith that makes men of will and thought persevere in spite of apparently insurmountable difficulties. They start with a strong confidence in the ultimate success of a noble undertaking and are, therefore, never daunted by difficulties, however formidable.

❖ Man is given faith in himself, his ideas and his powers that he may work and create and rise to greater things and in the end bring his strength as a worthy offering to the altar of the Spirit. All paralysing self-distrust has to be discouraged – all doubts in our strength to accomplish, an imagination of weakness and a denial of the omnipotence of the spirit.

❖ At the same time the aspirer should keep in mind the idea that his strength is not his own but that of the divine universal *Shakti*, and whatever is egoistic in his use of it must be a cause of limitation and in the end an obstacle.

– Sri Aurobindo

❖ Faith is the soul's witness to something not yet manifested, achieved or realised, but which yet the Knower within us, even in the absence of all indications, feels to be true or supremely worth following or achieving.

❖ Faith is an occult light and power from the soul amidst the mind's ignorance, doubts, weakness, incertitudes.

– Sri Aurobindo

Gems of Wisdom from Sri Sathya Sai Baba

- There is nothing like blind faith. In faith there can be no reason and no season. Faith and spirituality are beyond reason. Faith is the foundation for the realisation of God.

- Only a man of faith is completely free from fear. Love of God promotes fear of sin and makes one lead a moral life.

❖ Wipe out the root causes of anxiety — fear and ignorance. Anxiety is removed by faith in the Lord, the faith that tells you that whatever happens is for the best.

❖ When faith dawns, fence it around with discipline and self-control so that the tender shoot might be guarded against 'goats and cattle', the motley crowd of cynics and unbelievers. When your faith grows into a big tree, those very cattle can lie down in its shade.

❖ Faith can work wonders: it can compel the Lord to manifest himself and give you what you believe he will give you.

❖ Faith is said to be the "substance of things to be hoped for."

— *St Thomas Aquinas*

❖ When God gives us faith He enters into our soul and speaks to our spirit, not in the manner of discourse, but by way of inspiration, proposing in so sweet a manner unto the understanding that it moves the understanding to consent and yield to truth, without any doubt or distrust.

— *St Francis de Sales*

❖ A certain holy man has said, and we are glad to repeat it: 'The good fish is a godly faith. It lives among the waves and it is not broken or dissolved by them. Divine faith lives amidst the temptations and tempests of this world; the world rages, yet it remains uninjured.

— *St Augustine*

Faith – The Force of Life

- ❖ Faith is the force of life.

  – Tolstoy

- ❖ We walk by faith, not by sight.

  – The New Testament

- ❖ Faith means belief in something concerning which doubt is theoretically possible.

  – William James

- ❖ Faith does not depend upon experience; it is something that is there before experience.

  – Sri Aurobindo

- ❖ The faith waiting in the heart of a seed promises a miracle of life which it cannot prove at once.

  – Rabindranath Tagore

- ❖ I feel no need for any other faith than my faith in human beings.

  – Pearl S. Buck

- ❖ If you rely on God as he ought to be relied upon, He will provide for you as he provides for the birds; they go out empty and hungry in the morning and come back big-bellied at eve-tide.

  – Prophet Mohammad

❖ Understanding is the reward of faith. Therefore seek not to understand that you may believe, but believe that you may understand.

— St Augustine

❖ Faith without work cannot please, nor can good work without faith.

— St Bede the Venerable

❖ Sound faith is the beginning of a good life, of a life deserving of eternal life. Faith is to believe what we do not see; the reward of such faith is to see what we believe.

— St Augustine

The Bhagavad Gita

Threefold is by nature the inborn faith of the embodied — the good, the passionate and the dull. The Faith of each is shaped to his own nature, O Bharata, the man consists of his faith; that which his faith is, he is verily that.

— *Mind to Super Mind*
Rohit Mehta

One must watch over one's faith as one watches over the birth of something infinitely precious, and protect it very carefully from everything that can impair it.

In the ignorance and darkness of the beginning, faith is the most direct expression of the Divine Power which comes to fight and conquer.

— *The Mother*

"Just as the strong wind
has no hold upon a mighty rock,
so Mara has no hold
upon a man...
Who is endowed with unshakable faith and
who wastes
not his energies."

— The Dharmapada

Faith

Deep Faith

We must have faith that always what is for the best, happens. We may, for the moment, not consider it as the best because we are ignorant and also blind, and because we do not see the consequences of things which will happen later.

Faith through Aspiration

It is rare to have faith spontaneously, to be born with it. Aspiration can bring everything, provided it is sincere and constant. One always has a tiny element of faith within oneself, whether it be faith in what one's parents have said or in the books one has studied. After all, all your education is based upon a faith of this kind.

A Childlike Trust

The most important condition for faith is an almost childlike trust — the ability to say:

"What I need will be given to me; if I pray I shall have an answer; if I am in difficulty and ask for help, help will come — and not only will it come, but it will manage everything."

It is with the contradictions and doubts of the mind that one spoils everything and finally one builds a wall between oneself and the force one wants to receive. The psychic being has this trust, has it wonderfully, without a shadow, without an argument, without a contradiction. And when it is like that, there is not a prayer which does not get an answer, no aspiration which is not realised.

Watching Over One's Faith

Certainly a personal effort is needed to preserve one's faith, to let it grow within.

To sit down in inert passivity and say, "If I am to have faith I shall have it, the Divine will give it to me," is an attitude of laziness, of unconsciousness and almost of ill-will.

For the inner flame to burn, one must feed it; one must watch over the fire, throw into it the fuel of all the errors one wants to get rid of, all that delays the progress.

One must watch over one's faith as one watches over the birth of things infinitely precious, and protect it very carefully from everything that can impair it.

In the ignorance and darkness of the beginning, faith is the most direct expression of the Divine Power.

— *The Mother*

Faith and Trust
Both are Necessary

❖ Unless one adds to faith a total and complete trust in Divine Grace, there will be difficulties.

❖ Faith does not put any questions, does not think of the results : it gives itself entirely — it gives itself and then that's all.

Can Faith Increase by Personal Effort?

❖ Faith certainly is a gift given to us by Divine Grace. It is like a door suddenly opening upon an eternal truth, through which we can see it, almost touch it.

❖ Faith is the most direct expression of the Divine Power which comes to fight and conquers ignorance and darkness.

❖ Miracles always happen by faith.

But it all depends on your own standards and your sincerity, and the more you are physically ready, the more you are led to the right source, the right master. The psychic and its faith are always sincere. But if in your exterior being there is insincerity, and if you are seeking not spiritual life but personal powers, then that can mislead you. It is that, and not your faith, that misleads you. Pure in itself, faith can get mixed up in the being with low movements and it is then that you are misled.

— *The Mother*

The Power of Faith

❖ Man is the nature of his faith; what his faith is, that verily he is.

— *The Bhagavad Gita*

❖ Our hope is faint because our faith is weak.

— *Anon*

❖ He will not enter hell, who hath faith equal to a single grain of mustard seed in his heart.

— *Prophet Mohammad*

The Concept of Shraddha

> "Faith, sympathy, fiery faith and fiery sympathy : Faith, faith, faith in ourselves, faith, faith in God – This is the secret of greatness."
>
> – Swami Vivekananda

The Idea of Shraddha

- ❖ "*Shraddha*" is an Indian concept which Swamiji felt defied definition. According to him, the best illustration of *shraddha* is that which the young boy, Nachiketa of the Kathopanishad

had, when his father told him that he had been gifted to the god of Death.

- ❖ Unhesistatingly he went to the abode of Death and patiently waited at the door for the god of Death to appear. When the god appeared, Nachiketa started questioning him on the mystery of life and death. Not satisfied with the boons and knowledge he obtained, he requested Yama for the highest knowledge. Yama was not prepared to confer it that easily on the young boy. But Nachiketa persisted and at last, immensely pleased with his great *shraddha*, the god of Death conceded and imparted to him that immortal knowledge.

❖ Referring to this story, Swami Vivekananda said: "The idea of true *shraddha* must be brought back once more to us. Faith in our own selves must be awakened. What makes one man great and another weak is this *shraddha*. My master used to say: "He who thinks himself weak will become weak." That is true.

Some Notable Sayings

❖ Throughout the history of mankind, if any motive power has been more potent than another in the lives of all great men and women, it is that of faith in themselves.

❖ The old religions said that an atheist does not believe in God. The new religion says that he is an atheist who does not believe in himself.

❖ You know but little of that which is within you. For behind you is the ocean of infinite power and blessedness.

- ❖ Give up the awful disease that is creeping into our national psyche, that idea of ridiculing everything, that loss of seriousness.

- ❖ There are subjects where reason cannot take us far and we have to accept things on faith. Faith then does not contradict reason but transcends it.

- ❖ Without faith this world would come to nought in a moment. True faith is appropriation for the reasoned experiences of people whom we believe have lived a life purified by prayer and penance. Belief, therefore, in prophets or incarnations who have lived in remote ages is not an idle superstition but a satisfaction of an innermost spiritual want.

❖ A man without faith is like a drop thrown out of the ocean, bound to perish.

— *Mahatma Gandhi*

Faith and Confidence

❖ Whoever among devotees dedicates all acts to me, with no other thought, whoever meditates on Me, serves Me, worships Me, remembers Me, knows that I am always with him, ever providing for Him, I bear all his burdens and guarantee fulfilment of his needs and security.

— *The Bhagavad Gita*

❖ Faith in God means, faith that He is God, that He is Omnipresent, Omnipotent, Omniscient, and so on.

Confidence means trust in the word, will and work of God. You trust implicitly and blindly in the word, will, and act of God without any questions, doubts and uncertainties.

❖ When you have faith in God, He takes you under His shelter, protects you and will not let you suffer.

❖ Your FAITH in God will mitigate your suffering, determined as part of your duty (karma). In short, when you have hundred per cent faith, God in his compassion reduces your suffering, but He cannot reduce your karmas. Your karmas act as brakes and are binding on you. All the Lord does is to hand out Grace according to your karmas, according to what you deserve. In this way, you are bound and the Lord is entirely free.

❖ When you show cent per cent CONFIDENCE in God, He is totally bound to take care of you. No karmas of yours, whether good or bad can stand in the way and act as brakes.

❖ The power of total confidence is so great that it transgresses all karmas. It has the power of tying up God and completely binding Him in golden fetters, so that he is forced to bow down to the devotee and accede to his wishes and wants.

❖ Hundred per cent faith means that God will not let you suffer; hundred per cent confidence means that God will not let you down. Hundred per cent faith plus hundred per cent, confidence makes for hundred per cent devotion or *bhakti*. It is the highest form of *bhakti—paraabhakti* — where the Lord is in a state of golden bondage and the devotee is in a state of supreme serenity and smiling freedom. This is what every devotee has to aim at.

❖ You must remember here that faith and confidence are not two separate emotions. Without faith, there can be no confidence. If you do not have faith in someone, how can you have trust and confidence in him? So, faith comes first and then comes confidence. Faith is the seed, confidence is the sprout and devotion is the fruit.

❖ Just as you lean against the wall knowing that it will not collapse, lean on Him and depend upon Him entirely. He will then look after you and take care of everything for you. If you depend upon Him with complete faith and confidence, He shall provide for your welfare and look after all your needs in this world and in the next.

— *Sri Sathya Sai Baba*

- ❖ Faith is a function of the heart. It must be enforced by reason. The two are not antagonistic as some think. The more intense one's faith is, the more it whets one's reason.
- ❖ It is faith that steers us through stormy seas, faith that moves mountains and faith that jumps across the oceans. That faith is nothing but a living, wide-awake consciousness of God within. He who has achieved that faith wants nothing. Bodily diseased, he is spiritually healthy, physically poor, he rolls in spiritual riches.

– Mahatma Gandhi

The Extent of Grace

❖ No matter how great your faith and trust in Divine Grace, no matter how great your capacity to see it at work in all circumstances, at every moment, at every point in life, you will never succeed in understanding the marvellous immensity of its action, and the precision, the exactitude with which this action is accomplished; you will never be able to grasp the extent to which everything depends on Divine Grace.

Faith and Divine Grace

"Take refuge in him with
all thy heart;
through His Grace thou
shall attain supreme
Peace and Eternal Abode."

– The Bhagavad Gita

The Need for Grace

You must feel the need for Divine Grace. This is the most important point. It is to have a certain inner humility which makes you aware of your helplessness without Grace; that truly, without it, you are incomplete and powerless. This, to begin with, is the first thing. And then, if you become aware that it is only Grace which can do that which *you* cannot do, that Grace alone can pull you out of the situation in which you find yourself, can give you the solutions and the strength to come out of it, then, quite naturally, an intense aspiration awakes in you, a consciousness which is translated into an opening. If you call, aspire, and if you hope to get an answer, you will quite naturally open yourself to Grace.

— *The Mother*

- If birth, actions, youth, physical beauty, knowledge, etc., do not cause arrogance in any one, (know that) that is the sign of my Grace.
  － Lord Vishnu *"Sri Bhagvatam"*
- Three things are difficult to obtain, and if obtained, they are to be treated as a result of Grace of the Divine; these are: human birth, desire for spiritual emancipation and guidance and help from a *mahahpurusha*.
  － Shankracharya *"Viveka Chudamani"*

- Very right is thy faith and pride in His Grace, and true it is that it works like rain shower on a tilled field. But to what avail all shower, If ye have not sown the field!
  – *Sufi Sheikh Sa'di*

- His Grace may fall on us at any time. There is no definite rule regulating it. Some do not get it even after performing great austerities and night-long vigils, whilst it is forced on those who lie asleep!

– *Baba Farid (Sri Guru Granth Sahib)*

Even to turn towards God or strive towards liberation, man needs His Grace.

– Vedanta Philosophy

Success in life is a beautiful blending of self-effort and Divine Grace.

– Anon

Divine Grace only provides the occasion when total surrender becomes supreme victory.

– Anon

We sleep in peace in the arms of God when we yield ourselves upto His providence, in a delightful consciousness of His tender mercies; no more restless uncertainties, no more anxious desires, no more impatience at the place we are in; for it is God who has put us there, and who holds us in his arms. Can we be unsafe where He has placed us?

— Fenelon

He who can resign himself to the will of the Lord with simple faith and guileless devotion, attains Him without delay. He who has faith has all and he who lacks faith lacks all.

– *Sri Ramakrishna*